Sing and learn to the tune of Row, Row, Row Your Boat

Go, Go, Potty Time!

Potty & Toilet Training for Toddlers

Go, go, potty time,
for your pee and poo.

Sing along this song with us,
and you'll know what to do!

Dress, dress, dress yourself.
Do it every day.

Pulling up your underwear,
that is the toddler way!

Try, try, try it out,
to see just how it feels.

Climb aboard the potty train, straight after all your meals.

Feel, feel, feel the urge,
to have a poo or pee.

Your body tells you when it's time,
to sit on your potty!

Sit, sit, sit and wait,
upon the potty top.

Read a book or sing this song,
Until you hear a...

PLOP!

Ask, ask, ask for help.
An adult will help you.

Everybody needs to learn,
the way to pee and poo.

Wipe, wipe, wipe your bot.
Wipe it front to back.

It takes a while to get it right,
but soon you'll get the knack.

Flush, flush, flush away,
all the poo and pee.

Watch the water swirl around.
Clean toilet and potty.

Wash, wash, wash your hands,
when you poo or pee.

Use the soap and scrub them clean.
Now dry them 1-2-3!

Change, change, change your pants.
An accident perhaps.

Learning how to do it right,
will take a few mishaps.

BEST

BEST

Potty Training Progress Chart

	Mon	Tue	Wed		Thu	Fri	Sat	Sun
I listened myself	✕	✕						
I ask for my potty	✕	✕						
I did a wee or poop	✕	✕						
I did a poop or poop	✕	✕						
I wiped my bottom	✕	✕						
I washed my hands	✕	✕						
I was dry all night		✕						

BEST

BEST

Go, go, potty time,
for your pee and poo.

Now you've sung this song with us,
you sure know what to do!

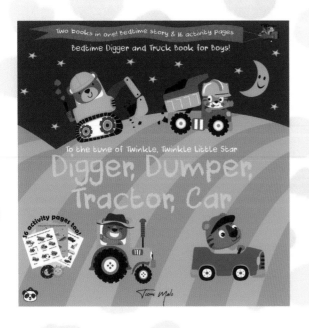

Thank you for reading my book!

I do hope you liked it enough to leave a review on Amazon as every one makes a huge difference to new authors like myself. I read every one as it helps me to create books you will enjoy.

Thank you so much! – Toomi

Please check out my other books on Amazon. Just search my name on Amazon or type Toomi.biz into your browser and it will redirect you to my Amazon author page.

As a student of Tibetan dream yoga and wellness practices, keeping a daily journal has had a life-changing positive impact on me. I only wish I had started younger, which is why I have created these journals for boys and girls.

These daily journals include sections that are very new to the West, like the practice of sending hugs to people we may have been in conflict with, to reduce stress and increase calmer sleep. I hope you will try them with your sons and daughters!

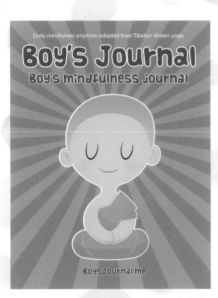

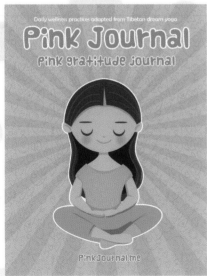

Potty Training Progress Chart

	Mon	Tue	Wed
I dressed myself			
I sat on my potty			
I did a wee on potty			
I did a poop on potty			
I wiped my bottom			
I emptied my potty			
I washed my hands			
I was dry all night			

Thu	Fri	Sat	Sun

Potty Training Progress Chart

	Mon	Tue	Wed
I dressed myself			
I sat on my potty			
I did a wee on potty			
I did a poop on potty			
I wiped my bottom			
I emptied my potty			
I washed my hands			
I was dry all night			

Thu	Fri	Sat	Sun

Potty Training Progress Chart

	Mon	Tue	Wed
I dressed myself			
I sat on my potty			
I did a wee on potty			
I did a poop on potty			
I wiped my bottom			
I emptied my potty			
I washed my hands			
I was dry all night			

Thu	Fri	Sat	Sun

Potty Training Progress Chart

	Mon	Tue	Wed
I dressed myself			
I sat on my potty			
I did a wee on potty			
I did a poop on potty			
I wiped my bottom			
I emptied my potty			
I washed my hands			
I was dry all night			

Thu	Fri	Sat	Sun

Potty Training Progress Chart

	Mon	Tue	Wed
I dressed myself			
I sat on my potty			
I did a wee on potty			
I did a poop on potty			
I wiped my bottom			
I emptied my potty			
I washed my hands			
I was dry all night			

Thu	Fri	Sat	Sun

Potty Training Progress Chart

	Mon	Tue	Wed
I dressed myself			
I sat on my potty			
I did a wee on potty			
I did a poop on potty			
I wiped my bottom			
I emptied my potty			
I washed my hands			
I was dry all night			

Thu	Fri	Sat	Sun

Printed in Great Britain
by Amazon